Everyday Service Excellence

Everyday Service Excellence

Simple Strategies for Outstanding Customer Service

George Houston

Everyday Service Excellence

ISBN: 9798344928760

DEDICATION

To my beautiful wife, Jay...

Thank you for loving and supporting me through every season of life.

Your unwavering faith in me has been my anchor, and I would not be

the man or father I am today without you by my side. You have the

biggest heart of anyone I've ever known, and you inspire me every day

to be better. Thank you for walking this journey with me, for every

laugh, every challenge, and every triumph we've shared.

To my amazing kids—Sarah Jane, Caleb, Timothy, Raleigh, Joseph, and

Elijah...

You have each taught me so much, more than words can say. I am

endlessly proud of who you are and who you're becoming. I believe in

each of you and know that you will make this world a better place.

Watching you grow has been my greatest joy, and I am honored to be

your father.

CONTENTS

INTRODUCTION

Everyday Service Excellence is a practical guide to elevate the way you approach customer service. Each chapter is designed to give you actionable steps that transform everyday interactions into moments that truly matter. Whether you're on the front line or in a leadership role, this book is here to help you create positive, memorable experiences with customers, one interaction at a time.

You'll learn how to build trust and loyalty, handle complaints with empathy, and approach challenges as opportunities for growth. Through core principles and simple techniques, you'll see how small, intentional actions can turn even difficult situations into chances to strengthen customer relationships. By consistently focusing on these fundamentals, great service can become second nature.

By the end of *Everyday Service Excellence*, you'll be equipped not only with practical skills but with a mindset that brings out the best in every customer interaction. This book is about making service excellence achievable and real in your daily work, allowing you to build a legacy that leaves others feeling valued, appreciated, and eager to return.

Everyday Service Excellence

CHAPTER 1

WHY GUEST SERVICE MATTERS

"IT IS NOT THE EMPLOYER WHO PAYS THE WAGES. EMPLOYERS ONLY HANDLE THE MONEY. IT IS THE CUSTOMER WHO PAYS THE WAGES."

- HENRY FORD

I'm a "why" kind of guy. All my life, whenever I've been told to do something (or not do something), I've always wanted to know the reason behind it. As a kid, I would sometimes get in trouble for asking my parents or teachers why. If you were like me, you probably got the same answer I did from most adults in authority. It often went something like, "... because I said so, that's why." As a parent now, I understand the popularity of this standard phrase—sometimes you just can't give a full explanation because a child wouldn't understand it. Other times, I've been guilty of using it because I was simply too tired to go into the details.

But as a kid, even if I didn't get a detailed answer, I still had questions. I wanted to understand why things were the way they were. Now, as an adult, I empathize with people who ask "why." So, when I became a manager at my restaurant, I hired a lot of teenagers and young adults, many of whom were working their first job. Just like any workplace, our restaurant had its share of rules and regulations— especially important in the restaurant industry, where health and safety standards are non-negotiable. Every time I hired and onboarded new team members, I did my best to remember my own curiosity as a kid. I tried to explain to them not just what we did but why we did it.

For example, if you're a new team member in a restaurant, one of the first jobs you'll likely do is washing dishes. I would start by showing them where we keep the dish soap, scrubbing pads, and how our dishwashing process worked. Then, I'd explain why it mattered that they did a thorough job with each dish. I'd ask if they planned on eating here and if they'd want to eat off a clean or dirty dish. I'd also ask if their friends or family might come here to eat and if they'd feel proud to serve them on dishes they'd washed. I'd emphasize that a clean kitchen isn't just a preference; it's essential for health and safety, as these are some of the things inspectors from the health department focus on when they visit. By explaining the "why" behind our expectations, I found new team members were more likely to buy into our goals and take pride in their work.

So, if you want to have great guest service at your restaurant, do you know why it matters? You must understand the *why* behind excellent guest service if you're going to provide it consistently. Working in a restaurant is a tough job with plenty of challenges, guest service being one of the biggest. But before you can improve your guest service, you need to understand the reason behind its importance.

This needs to understand "why" extends beyond the restaurant industry. In healthcare, for example, patient service is directly tied to both patient outcomes and satisfaction. When patients experience attentive,

compassionate service, they're more likely to trust their providers, leading to better adherence to treatment and overall satisfaction with their care.

In other industries, the impact of service quality is equally profound. In retail, friendly, knowledgeable customer service can be the difference between a one-time shopper and a lifelong customer. Successful retail brands have built their reputations on going above and beyond for customers, creating loyalty through exceptional service. In hospitality, whether it's a hotel, a cruise line, or a travel agency, great service creates memorable experiences, encouraging repeat visits and glowing reviews. In financial services, where products and services are often complex, customer service plays a key role in building trust. When clients feel valued and supported, they're more likely to stay loyal to their bank or financial advisor.

Now think about this: every few weeks, you receive a paycheck. You pick it up from your employer and deposit it at the bank. But who really gives you that paycheck? When I would ask my team members this question, I get all sorts of answers. Some say their manager gives them their paycheck, which is technically true. Others say it's the owners or CEO, and that's partially correct too. But these are only middle steps in the process. The real answer is the guest. Every dollar earned by the company comes from the guest spending their money with us. As Henry Ford said, "It is not the employer who pays the wages. Employers only handle the money. It is the customer who pays the wages."

When you and your team understand this concept—that the guest is essentially your paycheck—it makes sense why you'd want to provide great service. Imagine coming to work every day and delivering excellent guest service. Not only would you stand out to guests, but your dedication would also be noticed by coworkers and your boss. Want to make more money? Then approach your work with a focus on serving the guest. This effort will, over time, likely increase your paycheck.

How does that happen? First, as the company sees an increase in sales from repeat customers, there's more revenue to support raises and promotions. In turn the manager will likely schedule you for more hours if they see that you're dependable and provide exceptional service. Over time, this translates into higher paychecks and even potential

promotions, like moving into a supervisory role. On the other hand, if you neglect guest service, that too is noticed. Guests may choose to take their business elsewhere, reducing sales. This could ultimately lead to few hours on your schedule.

Since you're reading this book, it's clear you care about guest service, and fortunately, it's not overly complicated to excel at it. As I learned in Sunday School, the Golden Rule says, "Treat others the way you want to be treated." When you are a customer, you likely expect cleanliness, friendly, and timely service. Applying this standard to your work is the foundation of excellent guest service. It's about putting yourself in the guest's shoes and providing the experience you'd expect.

Throughout this book, I'll break down specific actions that can elevate your level of guest service. Remember, providing great service isn't just about what you do—it's about how you think. When you start to see your guest as your paycheck, it's easier to stay motivated and committed to delivering a great experience. Whether in a restaurant, a hospital, a hotel, or a bank, knowing the "why" behind service makes it easier to reach your service goals.

Everyday Service Excellence

CHAPTER 2

WHERE'S YOUR FOCUS?

"LIFE IS A MATTER OF CHOICES, AND EVERY

CHOICE YOU MAKE MAKES YOU."

- JOHN C. MAXWELL

If you've noticed so far in this book, I've chosen to use the word "guest" rather than "customer." This is intentional, because words matter. "Customer service" and "guest service" may seem interchangeable to most people, but they aren't quite the same. "Customer" implies a transactional interaction, where goods or services are exchanged. "Guest," however, goes deeper; it speaks to hospitality, welcoming, and accommodating, conjuring an image of someone we aim to make feel special and valued. Words matter, and the language we use shapes how we think and behave.

This distinction is not just a matter of semantics. It reflects a mindset: one that prioritizes treating each interaction as a personal experience rather than just a business transaction. This guest-first perspective can enhance service in any industry. In healthcare, for example, the shift from "patient" to "guest" creates an environment where the person receiving care feels valued beyond their treatment needs. Hospitals that emphasize a "guest" mindset—focusing on the experience of care, comfort, and individual respect—often see better patient satisfaction scores and outcomes. When healthcare workers view patients as valued guests, they bring empathy and attentiveness to the care they provide, building trust and fostering healing relationships.

The same principle applies in hospitality and retail. In high-end hotels, for instance, employees are trained to see each visitor as a guest, which prompts them to anticipate needs and create memorable experiences. Retail stores that treat shoppers as guests see higher loyalty and satisfaction, as customers feel appreciated rather than just another sale. Whether you're working in a restaurant, a clinic, a hotel, or a store, this focus on the guest has the power to transform interactions and deepen relationships.

So, when you're at work, make it your mission to keep the guest at the center of everything you do. Your focus should be serving the guest, meeting their needs, and creating a positive experience. As we discussed earlier, the guest is essentially your paycheck. Every dollar that supports your job comes from their choice to spend money with you. So, it's essential to keep this main goal front and center and not let other activities distract from it.

If you've worked in a restaurant for any length of time, you may have heard a manager say, "If you have time to lean, you have time to clean." Managers say this because of the unending list of tasks involved in running a restaurant—cleaning, restocking, and prepping. Daily operations require these tasks to ensure a smooth and efficient workflow. Think of all the activities you do to keep your restaurant clean and stocked up for busy periods. I'm sure you could list dozens of tasks needed to prepare for the rush.

However, while important, these checklists and tasks can sometimes overshadow the main mission of serving the guest. It's easy to get caught up in pre-closing routines or cleaning up to meet closing time deadlines, sometimes at the expense of guest attention. I've seen it in my own experience—moments when I was more focused on finishing a checklist than stopping to fully serve a guest's needs. When we let activities take precedence over guest satisfaction, it sends an unintended message: that our chores are more important than their experience.

To illustrate this point further, let's look at healthcare. Healthcare workers have countless tasks—documenting patient information, managing charts, and prepping for rounds. These tasks are essential, but if they take precedence over patient interaction, patients may feel ignored or undervalued. Similarly, in hospitality, hotel staff have their own set of behind-the-scenes responsibilities, but pausing to assist a guest always takes priority. If a front desk associate is too absorbed in paperwork to greet a guest warmly, the entire atmosphere suffers. In each of these industries, focusing on the guest over the task requires discipline and clear priorities. The difference between activities and results is clear: one keeps the organization running, while the other keeps the guests returning.

As a leader, you set the tone and focus for guest interactions. Completing tasks—whether they're cleaning, prepping, documenting, or organizing—is essential, but they can be scheduled or approached in ways that don't compromise guest attention. In many fields, timing is everything; tasks can often wait until guest interactions are minimal, and a quick, intentional pause to help a guest can make a lasting impact. Even during quieter moments, it's crucial to stay tuned to the guests who are there and to remember that their needs should come first.

Consider this: Are you more focused on the guest experience or on finishing your tasks? Are you demonstrating the guest-first mindset that you'd like others around you to adopt? It's not just about completing tasks but about being present and prioritizing in the moment. When your colleagues see you putting guests first, they're likely to follow your example.

Across industries, keeping the focus on the guest transforms routine interactions into exceptional experiences. Whether in healthcare, hospitality, retail, or any guest-centered field, choosing to focus on the guest first has a ripple effect that extends beyond individual interactions, building loyalty, satisfaction, and genuine connections. Ultimately, your

commitment to this mindset will set you apart, making both you and your organization stronger in the long run.

Everyday Service Excellence

CHAPTER 3

CHOOSING YOUR SERVICE

"People may forget what you said, but they will never forget how you made them feel." – Maya Angelou

In the service industry, every interaction with a guest is a pivotal moment. Whether you work in retail, healthcare, restaurants, or small businesses, you have a profound impact on the experience each guest has with your establishment. The choice to provide exceptional service is not just a part of your job description; it is a conscious decision you make every day. This chapter will explore how that choice shapes the guest experience and why it matters.

The Choice of Service

Every day begins with choices: Will you start your morning grumpy, or will you embrace positivity? This attitude doesn't just affect your mood; it influences every interaction you have with your guests. Regardless of your circumstances—whether you've had a rough night or are juggling personal issues—each time you step into your workplace, you have the power to choose your attitude and the quality of service you provide.

Consider the front-line roles in your organization, whether at a register, a reception desk, or in patient care. These team members face an immediate choice when the first guest or customer approaches. The decision to greet them with a smile, make eye contact, and offer genuine assistance sets the tone for the entire experience.

The service you provide reflects your commitment to that guest's happiness. A single negative interaction can deter a guest from returning, while a positive one can turn a first-time visitor into a loyal customer.

The Difference Between Activities and Results

In the fast-paced world of service, it's easy to get caught up in tasks—cleaning, organizing, and completing reports. However, activities should never overshadow the goal: guest satisfaction.

Ask yourself: What message are you sending when you prioritize tasks over service? When a guest is still enjoying their meal, yet a staff member is busy sweeping the floor or clattering dishes, it conveys that the activity is more important than the guest's experience. This can lead to misunderstandings, such as:

"Hurry up and leave; I have chores to do."

"Your comfort is secondary to my tasks."

"You shouldn't be here; it's closing time."

These messages undermine the essence of good service. The real purpose of any activity in a service environment should be to enhance guest comfort and satisfaction. If a task interferes with this outcome, it may need to be reassessed or rescheduled.

Consistency is Key

One of the most significant challenges in service is the need for consistency. You can't choose to provide exceptional service to only some guests and neglect others. Each guest deserves the same level of attention and care, regardless of their order or the time of day.

To create a great service experience, keep it simple: smile, maintain eye contact, and use courteous greetings. The key is to remain present and engaged, focusing on the individual in front of you rather than worrying about the next rush or your plans after work.

The Rewards of Choosing Good Service

When you choose to deliver good service, the benefits extend beyond the moment:

Happier Guests and Team Members: A positive atmosphere contributes to overall morale.

Easier Work Experience: Satisfied guests lead to less stress for staff.

Increased Loyalty: Happy guests are more likely to return, knowing they'll receive the same quality of service

Contagious Positivity: Your smile can inspire others, creating a ripple effect that enhances the entire environment.

Conversely, choosing poor service can have dire consequences:

Upset Guests and Team: A negative experience creates tension and dissatisfaction.

Reduced Patronage: Guests who leave unhappy are unlikely to return, impacting your business's bottom line.

Increased Workload: Recovering from bad service takes more effort than maintaining a positive atmosphere from the start.

Focus on the Guest

Ultimately, remember that your service impacts not just the guest's experience, but also your work environment. When activities distract from the goal of providing excellent service, both the guest and your team suffer.

Your mission—regardless of industry—is to create an

exceptional experience for every individual you serve. Your personal commitment to choosing great service will determine whether guests return and how your workplace feels.

What Choice Will You Make?

In the end, the choice to provide exceptional service is a decision that extends beyond just fulfilling job responsibilities; it is about creating memorable experiences for every guest. As Maya Angelou wisely stated, "People may forget what you said, but they will never forget how you made them feel." By consciously choosing to prioritize guest comfort and satisfaction, we not only enhance their experience but also pave the way for repeat visits. When we embrace the responsibility of making guests feel valued and appreciated, we transform ordinary service into extraordinary moments. Ultimately, it is this commitment to choice that determines whether guests will return and how positively they will remember their time with us.

Everyday Service Excellence

.

CHAPTER 4

IMPORTANCE OF TEAMWORK

"Great things in business are never done by one person;

they're done by a team of people." – Steve Jobs

Working as part of a team is more than simply dividing tasks; it's about building meaningful connections with others to accomplish a shared purpose. Across all industries—whether in a bustling healthcare facility, a customer service role, or a corporate office—three essential elements reinforce effective teamwork: respect, trust, and communication. Together, these qualities create a powerful foundation that drives high performance, enhances customer satisfaction, and strengthens team cohesion.

What is True Teamwork?

True teamwork isn't just about completing individual responsibilities; it emerges when individuals come together with a shared vision. Effective teams are defined by several key qualities: they have a shared purpose, clear goals, and an alignment of approaches. They willingly share information, support each other, and can constructively work through challenges.

At the core of each quality lies respect, trust, and communication—three essential values that define the nature of successful teamwork and shape positive interactions with customers, clients, and stakeholders.

Respect: The Foundation of Strong Teams

Respect is fundamental to any healthy relationship, and teamwork is no exception. It involves recognizing the unique contributions of each team member and interacting with kindness and professionalism. Respect is more than just an attitude; it's a series of actions that each team member practices daily:

Active Listening: Give others your full attention. Listening actively is one of the simplest yet most powerful ways to show respect.

Kind Communication: Tone and language matter; when we communicate with positivity and care, we promote a respectful atmosphere.

Appreciation and Accountability: Express gratitude when others contribute and take ownership of your own responsibilities. This sets a standard for maturity and collaboration within the team.

Constructive Feedback: Sharing insights respectfully and being open to feedback helps team members grow and feel valued.

Respectful interactions not only strengthen team dynamics but also improve the overall service experience. Customers and clients often sense when a team respects each other—resulting in a positive perception of the organization. In healthcare, for example, a culture of respect reassures patients, making them feel safe, valued, and heard.

Trust: The Heart of Teamwork

Trust is the glue that holds a team together, transforming a collection of individuals into a cohesive unit. It's about reliability, integrity, and open, honest communication. Teams that trust one another work more effectively, knowing they have each other's support. Trust in the workplace emerges from several key practices:

Reliability and Consistency: Following through on commitments and meeting expectations shows team members that they can depend on each other.

Honest Communication: Transparency and authenticity foster credibility and strengthen relationships.

Professionalism Over Judgment: Avoid gossip and assumptions. Staying focused on professionalism strengthens trust by showing respect for colleagues' integrity.

In any customer-oriented role, trust is critical. Customers are perceptive—they recognize when a team is unified and supportive, which reassures them about the service they'll receive. In a healthcare setting, trust among team members translates directly into patient safety and peace of mind.

Communication: The Bridge Between Respect and Trust

Communication is the channel through which respect and trust are built and maintained. Effective communication ensures that information flows smoothly and misunderstandings are minimized, making it easier for team members to work together and perform at their best. Here's how strong teams communicate:

Honesty with Empathy: Being direct yet empathetic, even during tough conversations, builds trust and sets a foundation of respect.

Active Listening and Responsiveness: Trying to understand each other's perspectives promotes respect and reduces conflict.

Solution-Oriented Feedback: A positive approach to problem-solving reduces tension and keeps the team focused on shared goals.

Effective communication directly impacts customer interactions, as well. Clients, patients, or customers can sense when there's a communication gap within a team, which can influence their perception of service quality. For example, clear, consistent communication among team members in a healthcare setting reassures patients that their care is in capable hands.

Handling Conflict Respectfully

Even in the best teams, conflicts can arise. Diverse perspectives and personalities occasionally lead to misunderstandings, yet the way conflicts are handled often strengthens a team. Here's how to approach conflict with respect:

Start Privately: When an issue arises, address it one-on-one to maintain professionalism and avoid tension.

Seek Help if Necessary: If a conversation doesn't resolve the issue, involve a manager to mediate in a respectful manner.

Keep a Professional Focus: Stay solution-oriented and find common ground. It's a chance to deepen respect and trust rather than weaken them.

Conflict, when managed well, can lead to a deeper understanding, innovative solutions, and stronger bonds among team members. This approach is invaluable in customer service and healthcare, where team unity directly impacts service quality.

Respect, Trust, and Communication in Customer Service

For any team to deliver exceptional customer service, these three pillars must be strong. Respect allows team members to collaborate harmoniously, trust fosters a sense of security for customers, and communication ensures that everyone is prepared to address customer needs effectively and professionally.

In any setting—whether a corporate office, a retail environment, or a customer service center—clients and customers notice how well team members work together. When they observe mutual respect, trust, and seamless communication, it builds confidence in the quality of service and reinforces loyalty and trust in the organization. A team that embodies these values can turn routine interactions into memorable experiences that keep customers coming back.

Embracing the Journey of Teamwork

Teamwork is a journey that requires each member to consistently practice respect, build trust, and communicate effectively. These principles don't just enhance individual contributions; they elevate the team. When teams align around respect, trust, and communication, they don't just function—they flourish.

Respect your teammates. Trust in each other's abilities. Communicate openly and honestly. By embracing these values, you'll become a stronger team member, helping to build a workplace that values everyone involved—whether they're on your team or on the receiving end of your service.

CHAPTER 5

KEEPING SERVICE SIMPLE

"Excellence is a standard that has no finish line."

– Quint Studer

In customer service, the simplest actions often make the biggest difference. Every day, we encounter guests with unique needs, preferences, and expectations, and our goal is to create "Encore Experiences"—moments so positive that guests want to return, bringing friends and family. While each guest may define a memorable experience differently, foundational elements like smiling, making eye contact, and using courteous language consistently elevate the customer experience.

This chapter, "Keeping Service Simple," is about embracing the essentials that are the foundation of every great service interaction. It's not about new tricks; it's about fully embracing the essentials that are at the core of each interaction. When practiced consistently, these elements can transform each interaction into a memorable one. We'll explore these components, then look at how the AIDET model from Quint Studer's *Hardwiring Excellence* helps create a structure for clarity and connection in service.

The Power of a Smile

A genuine smile is the universal expression of warmth, and it has a lasting effect on guests. A smile communicates to guests that they are welcome, valued, and that you're happy to serve them.

Why Smiling Matters

A smile is often the guest's first impression of you, and it sets a positive tone. When guests see a warm, friendly face, it can lift their mood and positively shape their entire experience.

Smiles are Contagious

Smiles have an amazing way of spreading positivity. Picture this: a guest walks in feeling stressed or preoccupied. But when they're greeted with a genuine smile, it's as if the weight of their day lifts, if only for a moment. That positivity can ripple out to other guests, team members, and even the broader environment. Imagine the effect when every team member embraces a positive attitude: it creates a warm, welcoming atmosphere that feels like a breath of fresh air. This is the positivity we want to spread around. Smiling consistently, even when we might not feel like it, can set off a wave of positivity that reaches everyone in the room.

Making Eye Contact

A meaningful connection starts with eye contact. When you look a guest in the eyes, you're letting them know you're fully present. Eye contact doesn't mean staring, but rather showing attentiveness in key moments.

Why Eye Contact is Essential

Eye contact signals respect and engagement. It tells the guest, "I see you, and I'm here to help." It's especially important during first impressions, as it reassures guests that they're being seen and heard. When a guest walks up to the counter, acknowledging them with direct eye contact and a smile creates a welcoming atmosphere that immediately sets them at ease.

Balancing Eye Contact for All Personality Types

If you're an introvert, making eye contact may feel challenging at first. Many of us prefer to focus on tasks, like looking at the register, computer, or notepad. But when you look up from your tasks to greet a

guest or ask a question, you're signaling that they're your priority. This

small gesture can make a big difference, even if it requires stepping out

of your comfort zone. For many introverts, adopting this habit

gradually helps it feel more natural and strengthens connections,

ensuring that each guest feels seen and valued.

Use of Pleasantries

Pleasantries are the "magic words" that can transform routine

interactions into extraordinary experiences. Simple phrases like

"please," "thank you," and "you're welcome" set a respectful tone,

conveying that you genuinely value the guest's presence.

Thanking Guests Frequently

In customer service, you can never thank guests too much.

Express gratitude when they place their order, when they receive their

items, and as they leave. This might seem repetitive, but for the guest, it reinforces a sense of gratitude and warmth. Avoid slang like "thanks" or casual responses like "no problem." Instead, use the full phrases "thank you" and "you're welcome" to maintain a professional and courteous tone.

Bringing It All Together: The AIDET Model

The AIDET Model, introduced in Quint Studer's *Hardwiring Excellence*, is a powerful framework that ensures every customer interaction includes clear and effective communication. AIDET stands for **Acknowledge, Introduce, Duration, Explain,** and **Thank You**. By following this framework, you ensure that each guest feels valued, informed, and appreciated, which is essential for creating a positive customer experience.

AIDET is designed to cover all elements of effective communication, helping guide interactions from start to finish. This structure serves as a checklist, ensuring that you don't miss any of the key touchpoints that make an experience memorable. It's useful across all types of interactions, whether it's welcoming a guest, handling a complaint, or providing information.

Acknowledge: Acknowledge everyone in the guest's group. Each person present plays a role in the experience, and even a simple smile or wave can let them know you're here to help. Taking the time to acknowledge everyone helps guests feel valued and welcome from the start.

Introduce: Introducing yourself by name or role builds immediate trust. A simple "Hi, I'm George, and I'll be helping you today" adds a personal touch, turning a standard interaction into a personal one. Introductions let the guest know who to turn to and build a rapport that can make them feel more at ease.

Duration: Wait times can be one of the biggest frustrations in any service interaction. When you estimate how long a guest might wait or how long the service will take, it reassures them that they're still a priority. If the duration extends, an update keeps them informed, eliminating the feeling of being forgotten.

Explain: You're an expert in your field, and the processes you follow may seem obvious to you, but that may not be the case for your guest. Take a moment to explain what you're doing. This transparency helps eliminate questions and builds trust, so the guest feels comfortable and informed throughout the interaction.

Thank You: Wrapping up the interaction with a sincere thank you is essential to creating a smooth transition for the guest. This simple act shows appreciation, reinforces that their time and trust are valued, and encourages them to return.

Keep It Simple

When it comes to service, the simplest actions often have the greatest impact. Smiling, making eye contact, using courteous language, and following the AIDET model are foundational to creating memorable guest experiences. Each interaction is a chance to make someone feel valued and respected. These simple yet powerful habits form the bedrock of exceptional service—an experience the guest will remember long after they've left.

By focusing on these basics and embracing the power of simplicity, you ensure that every guest leaves not only satisfied but truly impressed by their experience.

CHAPTER 6

THE ART OF EMPATHY IN SERVICE

"Empathy is the bridge to connection; it allows us to meet others where they are." – Brené Brown

Empathy isn't just a quality; it's a skill that can be refined and used to create positive, memorable experiences for guests. It's the ability to tune into what a person is feeling and needing, and it's at the core of exceptional service. In customer service, empathy transforms one-time visitors into loyal guests by making them feel seen, heard, and valued. This chapter will explore practical ways to develop empathy and show how it's the key to building rapport and trust.

Understanding the Value of Empathy in Service

Empathy goes beyond offering a smile and polite words. It's the difference between simply meeting a need and truly connecting with the guest. Guests can often feel vulnerable when they seek service—they may feel nervous, frustrated, or even embarrassed. Practicing empathy can help ease those emotions and put guests at ease, allowing you to help them better. When guests feel understood, they trust you, and that trust forms the foundation for an exceptional experience.

Let's break down some key empathy-building techniques and the steps you can take to become a more empathetic service provider.

Active Listening: Hear Beyond Words

Active listening is the foundation of empathy. Listening to a guest's words is only the first step; truly empathic listening requires attention to their tone, pace, and underlying emotions.

How to Practice Active Listening

Stay Focused: When a guest is speaking, put aside any other thoughts or distractions. Maintain eye contact, nod occasionally, and avoid interrupting.

Reflect: Summarize or rephrase what the guest has shared to show you've understood their needs. For example, if a guest says, "I'm really frustrated because my room wasn't ready when I arrived," you might reply, "I hear that you were expecting to be able to settle in right away, and this has disrupted your plans."

Ask Open-Ended Questions: These questions encourage guests to elaborate on their needs. For example, "Could you tell me more about what you're looking for?" shows you're interested in understanding them better.

Example: Active Listening in Action

Imagine a guest comes in visibly upset about a delay. They say, "This wait is unacceptable; I have somewhere to be!" Instead of rushing to apologize, take a moment to actively listen. "I understand you're in a hurry, and this delay is throwing off your schedule. Let me see how I can speed things up." By acknowledging both the problem and the guest's emotions, you're building empathy and trust.

Non-Verbal Cues: The Power of Body Language

Our words can only go so far; our body language often reveals what we really feel. For guests, a friendly gesture or a reassuring expression can convey empathy even before a single word is spoken.

Key Non-Verbal Signals for Empathy

Maintain Eye Contact: A warm, steady gaze shows that you're present and genuinely care about the guest's concerns.

Nod in Agreement: Simple nods at key points show that you're engaged and following along.

Smile Sincerely: A genuine smile is welcoming, but avoid smiling when a guest is upset, as it might seem dismissive. Instead, mirror their emotions to show empathy.

Example: Building Trust Through Non-Verbal Cues

Let's say a guest appears flustered because they can't find their way around. Instead of giving directions quickly and moving on, make eye contact, soften your expression, and listen as they explain. Offer to guide them if possible, walking them through the directions slowly and patiently. These small gestures can make a guest feel comfortable and valued.

Emotional Intelligence: Understanding and Regulating Emotions

Empathy is one component of emotional intelligence (EI), which is the ability to recognize, understand, and manage your own emotions and the emotions of others. In a high-stress environment, strong EI allows you to remain calm, control your response, and genuinely connect with the guest's experience.

Building Emotional Intelligence

Self-Awareness: Recognize your emotions as they arise and how they impact your actions. If you're feeling impatient, take a deep breath before responding to a guest.

Self-Regulation: Manage negative emotions that can cloud your empathy, such as frustration or stress. Learn to "reset" yourself between interactions to ensure each guest receives your full attention.

Empathy Development: Practicing empathy toward coworkers as well as guests can sharpen your skills and make empathy feel natural over time.

Example: Managing Emotions with EI

Imagine a guest is upset and raises their voice. Instead of taking it personally, acknowledge that the issue is important to them. Keep your own emotions in check and focus on addressing the problem, showing them that their experience matters to you.

Handling Difficult Emotions: Turning Conflict into Connection

When guests are unhappy, it can be challenging to remain empathetic, but it's precisely during these times that empathy is most powerful. Transforming a difficult situation into a positive one requires patience and the ability to address underlying emotions.

Steps for Handling Difficult Emotions

Acknowledge the Emotion: Start by identifying the guest's emotion—whether it's frustration, disappointment, or confusion.

Stay Patient and Calm: Let the guest vent if they need to. Often, they feel better after being given the chance to express themselves.

Show Genuine Concern: Use phrases like "I can see how frustrating that must be" to validate their experience.

Example: De-Escalating a Frustrated Guest

A guest might complain about a service delay, saying, "I expected more from your team." Instead of defending the delay, respond with empathy: "I understand that the wait has been frustrating, and that's not the experience we want for you. Let's make this right." This approach validates their feelings and refocuses the conversation on a solution.

Building Lasting Connections Through Empathy

When you approach each interaction with empathy, you help guests feel respected and valued, which strengthens their connection to your service. This sense of trust and connection encourages guests to return, and it may even inspire them to share their positive experiences with others. The result is a lasting impression that can transform a single interaction into a long-term relationship.

Empathy is not just a skill; it's a philosophy that can influence every aspect of customer service. It reminds us that every interaction is an opportunity to make someone's day a little better, a little easier, and a little brighter.

Empathy is the heart of exceptional service. By practicing empathy, you create an environment where every guest feels valued, respected, and understood. Whether you're solving a problem, handling a complaint, or simply engaging in friendly conversation, empathy is the bridge that allows you to connect with your guests and elevate their experience.

As Brené Brown wisely said, *"Empathy is the bridge to connection; it allows us to meet others where they are."* This bridge strengthens relationships, builds loyalty, and creates a memorable experience for every guest who crosses it.

CHAPTER 7

HOW TO BE FAST

"Efficiency is doing things right; effectiveness is doing the right things." – Peter Drucker

In today's fast-paced world, guests expect their needs to be met quickly and efficiently. With the rise of app-based ordering, delivery services, and curbside pickups, convenience is now a baseline expectation across service industries. This shift has increased the demand for quick and high-quality service, particularly in industries with drive-thru or high-volume service channels. For example, restaurants with a busy drive-thru lane know that a quick, well-organized system can help improve sales and maximize efficiency.

However, to stand out and foster customer loyalty, speed alone is not enough—you need to be truly F.A.S.T.

In this chapter, we'll break down what it means to be F.A.S.T.: Friendly, Accurate, Safe, and Trained. Together, these qualities create a seamless guest experience that is not only efficient but leaves a lasting positive impression.

Friendly

The first element of being F.A.S.T. is friendliness. Any business can provide quick service, but a friendly touch goes a long way in setting your team apart from the competition. In a restaurant drive-thru, for example, the guest may only interact with one or two team members, but these brief interactions leave a lasting impression of your brand.

Imagine you pull up to a drive thru. You're ready to order, but instead of a warm greeting, you're met with a robotic voice or, worse, silence. When you arrive at the window, the employee barely acknowledges you, handing over your food without so much as a smile or "thank you." This type of impersonal service can leave a sour taste, making customers hesitant to return.

In a healthcare clinic, patients are often anxious or in a rush. A receptionist who looks up from the desk, makes eye contact, and offers a smile with a simple, "How can I help make you today?" can set a reassuring tone. This can be done quickly but effectively, giving the patient a sense of comfort.

Think of a clothing store during a holiday season. The lines are long, and customers are rushing. A friendly cashier who maintains a cheerful attitude and thanks customers when handing back receipts or cards can make even a fast transaction feel personalized.

As a leader, setting a friendly tone starts with you. When you model friendly behavior, your team is more likely to follow suit. A brief pre-shift meeting can be a great way to get the team energized, review goals, and establish expectations for the shift. Encourage team members to smile, even when they're speaking on the phone or through headset; customers can "hear" the smile, which makes a surprising difference in the quality of their experience.

Key Takeaway: It's not enough to be fast; you must be friendly, too.

Accurate

Speed means little if the service isn't accurate. There's nothing more frustrating for a guest than waiting in line only to discover their order is incorrect. This common issue can be especially prevalent in fast-paced environments where there's pressure to keep things moving. Imagine getting your coffee only to realize it's the wrong order. Suddenly, all that time saved by quick service goes out the window because now you need a correction.

When accuracy is prioritized, guests feel confident that their orders will be right the first time. It's important to remember that consistency is often built through repetition and strong, reliable processes. Just as a musician practices scales or a sports team runs drills, service accuracy improves with practice and attention to detail.

Establish a "correctness-first, quickness-second" mindset within your team. When your employees are properly trained in the steps and procedures needed to prepare orders, speed becomes a natural byproduct of experience and precision. During a holiday rush, it's easy for cashiers to make mistakes in transactions. However, accuracy in scanning items, applying discounts, and giving the correct change ensures the experience is hassle-free. Even if lines are moving quickly, maintaining accuracy builds trust with customers.

Additionally, clean, organized workspaces are essential for accuracy. Mistakes are more likely to happen if team members are scrambling to find what they need then. By keeping workstations well-organized, the team can be more efficient and focused, ensuring orders are correct every time.

Key Takeaway: It's not enough to be fast; you must be accurate.

Safe

In a high-speed environment, it's tempting to cut corners for the sake of saving time. However, no amount of speed can justify compromising safety. Safety isn't just about preventing injuries in the workplace; it's also about maintaining a standard that customers can trust. In the food service industry, for instance, customers expect that their meals are prepared in clean, sanitized conditions. If your team rushes through food prep and ignores safety protocols, it puts both the team and the customers at risk.

Often, the drive-thru or front-line employees get the spotlight for speedy service, but the back-line team is equally important in ensuring safe, clean, and well-prepared food reaches the customer. Emphasize to your team that every role is essential, and everyone should feel empowered to prioritize safety.

Healthcare workers are often under intense time pressure. However, even when working quickly, following correct protocols for things like sterilization and patient data privacy is crucial to patient safety and quality care.

Safety protocols are there for a reason, and as a leader, it's your responsibility to reinforce them regularly. If the environment feels rushed, remind team members that while speed is important, safe practices are non-negotiable. In the long run, a safe workplace is more productive and sustainable.

Key Takeaway: It doesn't matter how fast you are if you aren't safe.

Trained

Finally, the "T" in F.A.S.T. stands for Trained. A well-trained team is the backbone of an efficient, friendly, accurate, and safe operation. Training goes beyond just initial orientation; it's a continuous process that keeps skills sharp and prepares team members for both routine tasks and unexpected challenges.

Guests notice when they're served by someone knowledgeable and confident in their role. Whether it's in a restaurant, healthcare facility, or retail store, guests are put at ease by competent employees who know how to handle their requests and solve problems. Proper training equips your team with the skills they need to provide great service and the confidence to perform well under pressure.

Training should cover both technical skills, like preparing food or handling customer transactions, and soft skills, like communication and problem-solving. As a leader, create a culture where learning is valued. Offer opportunities for cross-training so team members can handle a variety of roles. This not only makes your operation more flexible but also builds team members' confidence, as they feel capable and prepared.

At a technology store, an employee who is trained on the latest devices can answer customer questions more effectively and speed up sales. They can assist customers confidently without needing to call a manager, reducing wait times and boosting the customer's experience.

In a healthcare setting, training is critical. Receptionists who are cross trained on billing, insurance verification, and patient triage can handle a greater range of requests without needing to pass tasks on to other team members, ultimately making the service faster and more convenient for patients.

In a busy coffee shop, a barista with proper training can prepare multiple orders efficiently without sacrificing quality. Knowing the menu, understanding how to use equipment, and being skilled at making drinks can help them serve quickly and accurately without getting flustered.

Periodic refresher sessions are another great way to ensure that standards are maintained and any changes in procedure are clearly communicated. Shadowing, role-playing exercises, and even mystery shoppers can help you identify areas where additional training might be beneficial. Remember, a trained team is a prepared team—and a prepared team is what enables a truly F.A.S.T. operation.

Key Takeaway: A fast operation depends on well-trained employees who can confidently and effectively serve guests.

In the end being F.A.S.T. isn't about sacrificing quality for speed; it's about creating a seamless experience that leaves customers satisfied and eager to return. By focusing on being Friendly, Accurate, Safe, and Trained, your team can deliver an experience that feels effortless, dependable, and personable. In a world where speed is often a given, these four principles will help your business stand out for its excellence.

"Efficiency is doing things right; effectiveness is doing the right things."

– Peter Drucker

CHAPTER 8

THE POWER OF PRECEPTION

"You never get a second chance to make a first impression."

— Will Rogers

When I was a teenager, I remember seeing a commercial for Head & Shoulders shampoo that left an impression on me—and not just because of the product. In the ad, a guy wanted to ask a girl out on a date. He worked up his nerve, but she turned him down. His friend, noticing flakes on his shoulder, handed him a bottle of Head & Shoulders shampoo. The screen cut to him using the shampoo, and then the announcer's voice came in with a line I'll never forget: "You never get a second chance to make a good first impression." In the final scene, he and his friend were cruising in a convertible, off to a double date.

This ad stuck with me because it highlighted a truth, we all know well: first impressions matter. And the truth is, we're all experts at creating first impressions, whether we realize it or not. Think back to your first day of school. You probably spent time deciding what to wear, making sure you had all your school supplies—after all, you only had one chance to make that first impression on your new classmates and teachers.

Or maybe you remember preparing for your first date. You made sure your clothes were right, that you smelled good, and maybe even planned what to say ahead of time. Every little detail felt crucial because, deep down, you knew that how you presented yourself in those first few minutes would shape the other person's view of you. After all your goal was to have the option of a second date.

The same goes for a job interview. You iron your clothes, check your hair, and think through answers to potential questions. You arrive on time—maybe even a few minutes early—because you want to show that you're responsible, reliable, and serious about the opportunity. All this preparation is built around one goal: to make the best possible impression right from the start.

Understanding Perception

So, what is perception? Perception is our recognition and interpretation of sensory information, drawn mostly from memory and experience. It's the insight or intuition we have when we interpret someone or something around us. And in the service industry, perception is reality.

People come to you not just for help but for the whole experience. Whether in food service, healthcare or any other service industry, people are looking for more than just efficiency or professionalism; they want to feel seen, valued, and respected. This feeling is directly connected to their perception of your business, shaped in large part by how you make them feel.

The Double-Edged Sword of First Impressions

First impressions, though, are a double-edged sword. They have the power to make or break you in an instant. A great first impression can set you up for success, opening doors and building relationships. But a bad one? That can stick with you, shaping people's perceptions of you for a long time. When it's negative, it can be difficult—sometimes impossible—to shake off and repair your reputation. This is why the effort you put into every interaction, especially that first one, is so critical.

Remember, we're not just experts in making first impressions for ourselves; in the service industry, every interaction is a chance to create a positive experience and shape someone's perception of our entire organization.

Areas of Perception

Perception is shaped by many factors, but in the service industry, two areas stand out: the facility and the staff. Together, they shape a guest's overall experience, often determining whether they'll return and what they'll say to others about the experience. Let's dive deeper into how each area affects perception.

The Facility

Guests immediately notice the environment they walk into, and the facility's cleanliness, décor, and atmosphere play a big role in shaping their first impression. From the moment they enter, they subconsciously evaluate everything around them. Here are the main aspects they focus on:

Cleanliness: This is foundational. Whether it's the waiting area, restrooms, or service spaces, a clean environment conveys respect, professionalism, and a commitment to quality. Dusty surfaces, trash, or an unkempt space quickly undermine trust and comfort. People are more likely to feel at ease and welcomed in a spotless space.

Décor and Ambiance: Décor goes beyond mere aesthetics; it influences how people feel while they're there. Lighting, color schemes, furnishings, and even music all play a part. A well-thought-out ambiance can make guests feel relaxed and valued, whereas poor design choices or outdated décor might create a perception of neglect or complacency.

Efficiency of Layout and Flow: Guests appreciate spaces that are easy to navigate, with clear directions and well-thought-out layouts. A chaotic or crowded setup often causes frustration, making it difficult for guests to feel comfortable or attended to. A streamlined environment, by contrast, can reduce stress and improve the overall experience, making people feel more in control and less like they're "just another customer."

The Staff

As impactful as the facility is, it's the staff who truly bring the experience to life. The team's behavior, attitude, and appearance serve as direct reflections of the organization's values and culture. For most guests, the way staff members engage with them is the most memorable part of their visit and has a lasting effect on their perception.

Attitude and Approachability: From the way staff greet guests to how they handle questions or issues, their attitude speaks volumes. A warm smile, a willingness to help, and a calm, attentive demeanor helps guests feel seen, heard, and valued. On the other hand, indifference or a rushed, impersonal interaction can leave a negative impression, even if the staff member is otherwise efficient. Guests remember how the staff made them feel, often more than any other part of the experience.

Professional Appearance: Professionalism in appearance signals respect for guests and a commitment to quality. Whether it's a uniform or business attire, looking polished and prepared reassures guests that they're in capable hands. A sloppy or inconsistent appearance can unintentionally suggest that standards are lacking, leaving guests questioning the overall quality of the service.

Empathy and Adaptability: Being able to adapt to each guest's unique needs, moods, and expectations is a skill that truly sets great staff members apart. Guests often come with different emotions and backgrounds, and when staff show empathy—by actively listening and adapting their approach— they build rapport and make the experience memorable. This adaptability is especially important when handling difficult or unexpected situations, as it shows guests that the staff can manage anything with professionalism and care.

Why These Areas Matter

Each area—facility and staff—reinforces the other. A clean, well-designed environment builds the initial impression, setting the stage for the interactions that follow. When the team embodies friendliness, professionalism, and empathy, they elevate the entire experience, turning first-time visitors into loyal guests.

Perception is powerful because it's not just about what people see; it's about how they feel. Every detail, whether in the environment or in a staff interaction, contributes to the perception guests take away with them. These details, while sometimes small, can determine whether the perception is one of excellence and trustworthiness or one of disappointment and disregard.

How Does AIDET Help with Perception?

AIDET is a communication framework that helps create consistent, positive interactions in any service industry. It covers five key areas, each of which builds trust, reduces anxiety, and enhances perception.

Acknowledge

Make every guest feel noticed. Simply acknowledging someone

with a smile or a wave sets a welcoming tone, signaling that you're here to help.

Body Language & Tone – Being self-aware when a guest walks in or passes by communicates openness and respect.

Introduce

Taking a moment to introduce yourself helps build trust. Adding your role and a bit about your experience can enhance your credibility, while letting guests get to know you fosters friendliness and compassion.

Duration

Waiting times can be a primary source of guest frustration. Setting clear expectations about wait times and providing occasional updates reassure guests that they're still a priority and haven't been forgotten.

Perception of Wait Times – Remember that the feeling of waiting often impacts guests as much as the actual wait. Finding ways to communicate even during wait times is key to positive perception.

Explain

In any service role, you're the expert. However, what's second nature to you may be unfamiliar to a guest. Taking time to explain what you're doing eases concerns and builds trust, especially in complex or technical interactions.

Who Gets the Best Service of the Day? – The customers at the begging or the end of your shift? It's easy to slip into autopilot, especially with routine tasks. But by taking a bit of extra time with each guest, you ensure everyone feels respected and valued, which leads to positive perception.

Thank You

Guests are often dealing with uncertainty, whether in healthcare or another service setting. A genuine "thank you" can convey appreciation, humanize the interaction, and make people feel more at ease.

Perception and Service: Putting It All Together

The goal of AIDET is to decrease anxiety and improve

outcomes by creating positive perceptions. When guests feel valued and

cared for, they are more likely to have a favorable impression, and

positive experiences foster loyalty.

Formula:

- Negative Service = Negative Perception = Negative Outcomes

- Positive Service = Positive Perception = Positive Outcomes

Using The AIDET Model as a consistent approach can create a

powerful, positive perception.

Perception of Team Members

People are more influenced by personalities and moods than by

anything else. Your appearance, your energy, your attitude—they all

play a huge role in how customers perceive your workplace. When you're on duty, you're not just representing yourself; you're representing your whole team and the values of your organization.

Customers notice everything, from how you present yourself to how hard you're working. They form opinions based on your demeanor, professionalism, and friendliness. A warm, friendly environment doesn't just call for clean uniforms; it calls for warm, friendly service. A little extra effort in every interaction—showing kindness, patience, and positivity—can make your team look exceptional, even in challenging situations.

Bringing It All Together

Every interaction is an opportunity to create a positive perception. When you're intentional about first impressions and consistent in your service, you build a lasting reputation for excellence. AIDET helps by decreasing customer anxiety and increasing trust, both of which lead to better outcomes.

In service, we're more than our job roles; we're a critical part of the experience our customers walk away with. And in the end, their perception of us will determine how they feel, whether they'll return, and what they'll tell others.

CHAPTER 9

WHAT TO DO WHEN THINGS GO WRONG

"A complaint is a gift, a second chance to improve and earn loyalty." – Janelle Barlow

The action you or a team member takes to correct a potentially unhappy situation is called service recovery. It's one of the most powerful moments to build loyalty, transforming a negative experience into one that strengthens the guest's trust and satisfaction. Although it's not possible to prevent every problem a guest might encounter, you can always make it right when something does go wrong. A successful service recovery can turn an angry guest into a loyal one—possibly even more loyal than if the experience had gone perfectly in the first place.

When a complaint is brought to your attention, it's essential to respond immediately and handle it with care. Effective service recovery follows a consistent approach, whether the complaint arrives in person, at the drive-thru, over the phone, or through a feedback form.

One core practice in handling complaints is showing sincere empathy by saying, "I'm sorry" at least three times during the interaction. First, apologize when the complaint is made known. Then, before you correct the issue, say it again to reinforce your understanding of their frustration. Finally, repeat it once the problem is resolved to communicate a sense of completion and appreciation. This approach ensures that the guest feels genuinely heard and valued at each stage of the interaction. Sometimes, when people are upset, their anger can cloud their ability to listen. By reinforcing your empathy, you're helping them see your commitment to making things right.

In all complaints, it's crucial for the manager to apologize sincerely. When you say, "I'm sorry" or "I'm sorry this happened to you," you're not necessarily accepting blame but rather showing genuine empathy. Imagine a friend telling you they were caught in the rain without an umbrella. A natural response might be, "Oh, I'm sorry you had to go through that." You didn't cause the rain, but you can understand the inconvenience. In service recovery, your empathy shows that you understand the guest's frustration and are committed to helping them move forward with a positive impression.

The Five Steps to Service Recovery

Whenever I'm called to address an upset guest, I follow a simple yet effective approach: Listen, Repeat, Thank, Apologize, and Act.

1. **Listen** – Hear the guest out entirely, giving them space to express their feelings. Often, feelings are more important than the words they use. Don't interrupt—just listen. Many times, simply being heard can resolve most of their frustration, as it makes them feel seen and valued.

2. **Repeat** – After listening, summarize back what you understood. This ensures that you're clear on the specifics of their complaint, and it reassures the guest that you were paying close attention to what they shared. Repeating also reinforces their feeling of being heard.

3. **Thank** – This step may seem surprising, but it's powerful. By genuinely thanking the guest for bringing the issue to your attention, you demonstrate that you see their complaint as an opportunity to improve. The right tone can turn an intense conversation into a productive one, helping the guest feel appreciated for their input.

4. **Apologize** – As we discussed, saying "I'm sorry" at least three times throughout the interaction solidifies your empathy. Here, you can repeat it to acknowledge the guest's frustration directly and validate their experience.

5. **Act** – Show them that you're committed to fixing the issue. Explain what steps you're going to take and, if possible, what you'll do to prevent the issue from happening again. Acting

assures the guest that you're willing to invest time and effort in their satisfaction.

These five steps—Listen, Repeat, Thank, Apologize, and Act—provide a reliable way to handle complaints, ensuring that each interaction feels personalized and responsive. When your team embraces these steps, they're not just fixing problems; they're building trust and creating loyal advocates for your business.

The Power of a Second Chance

Every complaint offers a unique opportunity—a second chance to show a guest that they matter. When handled well, addressing an issue not only restores their experience but can deepen their trust and loyalty. As Janelle Barlow wisely said, "A complaint is a gift, a second chance to improve and earn loyalty." By responding with empathy, gratitude, and action, you're demonstrating to the guest that your commitment to their satisfaction goes beyond any one interaction.

While not every situation is easy, the effort to listen, acknowledge, and make things right can transform even the most challenging experiences into moments of connection. In service recovery, every action you take reinforces the idea that their experience—and loyalty—are valuable to you.

CHAPTER 10

EMBRACING EXCELLENCE EVERYDAY

"The best way to find yourself is to lose yourself in the service of others." – Gandhi

In the journey to provide exceptional customer service, the knowledge, skills, and techniques you've gained are only as powerful as the mindset you adopt. Exceptional service is more than a set of tasks; it's a way of thinking, a habit of caring, and a personal commitment to go above and beyond for every individual you serve. This final chapter is a call to embrace excellence every day by integrating the principles you've learned into who you are as a service professional, teammate, and leader.

Commitment to a Service Mindset

Great service isn't just about the actions you take—it's a mindset that becomes part of your identity. A service-first attitude means viewing every interaction as an opportunity to create positive, memorable experiences. When you adopt this mindset, you don't just respond to needs; you anticipate them. You become more empathetic, perceptive, and proactive, capable of transforming routine interactions into meaningful connections.

Adopting a service mindset can have a profound impact, not only on customer satisfaction but on your relationships and career trajectory. The dedication you bring to each interaction builds trust, fosters loyalty, and earns respect. By choosing to embrace service excellence every day, you're not only enhancing the experience for others—you're also setting a standard for yourself that will elevate your professional journey.

Taking Small, Intentional Steps

Great service is achieved through small, intentional actions that, over time, have a powerful cumulative effect. Every interaction is an opportunity to put the principles you've learned into action: friendliness, accuracy, safety, and attentiveness. These seemingly minor choices add up, creating a reputation for excellence that others recognize and value.

You now have a toolbox filled with practical skills and strategies to make every interaction count. Whether it's a smile, a thoughtful follow-up, or the extra care taken to ensure accuracy, these small efforts become the foundation of an outstanding service experience. Remember, being truly exceptional isn't about grand gestures; it's about consistency and intentionality, which together lay the groundwork for lasting impact.

Call to Action: Creating Your Service Legacy

Now, it's time to act. You've learned what it takes to provide exceptional service, but the journey doesn't stop here. Embrace this call to action: choose one principle each week for the next two months and commit to practicing it. Track your progress, reflect on your growth, and even invite your team to join you. Share your successes, learn from your challenges, and see the impact that these efforts create, not only in your workplace but in every area of your life.

By consistently embodying these principles, you're not just achieving a level of personal excellence—you're building a legacy of service. Imagine the ripple effect of your commitment: teammates inspired by your example, customers who feel valued, and a community uplifted by your dedication to excellence. This is the impact of a service-first mindset.

As you close this chapter, remember Gandhi's words: "The best way to find yourself is to lose yourself in the service of others." When you commit to this mindset, you gain more than just professional success—you find a sense of purpose, fulfillment, and connection. Let service be your compass, guiding you toward a legacy of meaningful impact that resonates far beyond any single moment or interaction.

ABOUT THE AUTHOR

With nearly two decades in HR & Training and Development, George Houston brings a unique blend of experience, passion, and insight to the field of customer service. His career spans manufacturing, healthcare, and food service—industries where he has aligned HR strategies with operational goals, ensuring both employee success and organizational growth. As a lifelong learner and advocate for personal development, George is dedicated to empowering others to reach their highest potential.

Beyond the workplace, George's commitment to growth extends to his personal life. He is happily married to Jay, the love of his life, and together they are raising six incredible children. Whether he's watching football and baseball, playing guitar, or coaching youth sports in the evenings, George's passion for guiding and inspiring others shines through.

This book reflects George's drive to create a meaningful impact. It's his invitation to readers to embrace a service mindset, unlock new levels of professional and personal success, and bring excellence into every interaction.

www.ingramcontent.com/pod-product-compliance
Lightning Source LLC
Chambersburg PA
CBHW071522220526
45472CB00003B/1119